G000140747

'This book will bear comfort to the sick and wisdom to caregivers and ministers. Father Éamonn writes honestly, boldly letting the ill know that he honours and understands their real condition. And by leading them into reality, Fr Éamonn knows he is leading the reader into a prayerful engagement with God. Settled into reality, the reader will reap its benefit, becoming more and more vulnerable to the divine physician.

'Give this book to every priest and deacon you know. Pray with this book in the presence of every suffering person you know and let the grace that it carries unfold.'

Deacon James Keating, PhD
Professor of Spiritual Theology,
Kenrick-Glennon Seminary, USA

'The great gift of Fr Éamonn's book is that it is so real and compassionately invites us to be real in our prayer. Very powerful, encouraging and liberating for any of us living with illness.'

Father Ciarán Enright
Parish priest, Archdiocese of Dublin

Master, the One You Love is Ill

Reflections on Illness and Caring for the Sick

Fr Éamonn P. Bourke

VERITAS

Published 2021 by
Veritas Publications
7–8 Lower Abbey Street
Dublin 1
Ireland
publications@veritas.ie
www.veritas.ie

ISBN: 978 1 84730 984 6

A catalogue record for this book is available from the British Library.

Designed and typeset by Padraig McCormack, Veritas
Printed in the Republic of Ireland by Walsh Colour Print, Kerry

Veritas books are printed on paper made from the wood pulp of managed forests. For every tree felled, at least one tree is planted, thereby renewing natural resources.

Contents

Introduction

Shouting and screaming, in silence and in tears may be the only ways that we can pray during times of illness. At one stage or another in our lives, illness may come to our door. Whether young, middle aged or older, its impact on our lives can be inconvenient at best and debilitating and shocking at worst. We know how difficult it can be at times to pray even when things are good and we are feeling well. When we are afflicted by illness and infirmity, it can be all the more difficult to find the strength, the energy and the words we need to pray.

Illness comes not only with physical effects, but also has a deeply spiritual dimension. Pope Francis, speaking about the Covid-19 pandemic from an empty St Peter's Square on 27 March 2020, summed up the atmosphere surrounding the virus when he said, 'We find ourselves afraid and lost.' We can use these same words to describe what happens when we find ourselves plunged into illness. As we are affected physically, mentally, emotionally and spiritually, we can feel afraid and lost.

Prayer during times of illness can seem nigh on impossible as we try to muster up the strength just to keep going. It is at times like these that we realise through the scriptures that we are not alone, not abandoned, and that we do not need to feel afraid or lost. Christ is our strength. Christ is our stronghold. Christ is our healer. As he was with the blind, the lame and the deaf, so too is he with us. As he reached out to heal the eyes of the blind, so too he reaches out to heal us. The ferocity of the waves that struck the boat of the disciples on the Sea of Galilee can mirror the ferocity of illness on the shores of our lives. And yet Christ is in the boat with us – if we can only stop and take the time to recognise his healing presence.

The simple reflections ahead take the reader through the byways of the Holy Land to meet the Lord Jesus who seeks out the lost, the lonely and the ill. They are real stories of encounter with the Messiah, the Saviour of the World. These reflections illustrate the healing power of the Lord who shows the deepest compassion to those whose lives have been turned upside down due to illness. Hopefully, these reflections will throw some light onto your own experience of illness and help you navigate through the turbulent waters of infirmity, taking you to the place of encounter with your God.

Read the scripture pieces slowly. Imagine the scenes. Imagine what it must have been like for the characters in each story. Try to understand the enormity of each person's illness and the effect it was having on their life. Try to understand the efforts they, or others, made to get to Jesus the healer. See how Jesus lovingly treats each sick person with dignity and respect. Try to understand the impact meeting Jesus had on the person's illness and their life. Try to put yourself in the place of the sick person and consider, from your own unique experience of illness, how you might react to Christ as he approaches you. What would you say to Jesus? What would you want him to do for you?

It is hoped that these reflections might touch in some way the reality of your sickness. As you read them, try doing so with a pen and paper handy so that you can take note of the unique inspirations the Holy Spirit offers to you. Take these inspirations to prayer. Allow the power of the Spirit to enlighten you to the real presence of Christ who is Immanuel, God with us. May the healing Christ touch the eyes of your mind to see what hope his call holds for you.

1. 'Why Have You Forsaken Me?'

The Death of Jesus
Matthew 27:45–50

From noon onward, darkness came over the whole land until three in the afternoon. And about three o'clock Jesus cried out in a loud voice, *'Eli, Eli, lema sabachthani?'*, which means 'My God, my God, why have you forsaken me?' Some of the bystanders who heard it said, 'This one is calling for Elijah.' Immediately one of them ran to get a sponge; he soaked it in wine, and putting it on a reed, gave it to him to drink. But the rest said, 'Wait, let us see if Elijah comes to save him.' But Jesus cried out again in a loud voice, and gave up his spirit.

What line or phrase stands out for you as you read this passage? Take a quiet moment to dwell on this line or phrase, asking the Holy Spirit to heal you through it.

Reflection

When things are going well in life it can be very easy to pray. When the horizon is clear and there are no present or immediate challenges, prayer often flows and we can find words that easily express this warm and pleasant period. We can call this time a time of consolation – when we can feel the presence of God in an easier way and there are no real or present challenges or dangers to our health. We give thanks for these times. We rejoice in these times.

However, what happens when we are challenged, when the horizon seems swamped with clouds and we cannot easily see the road ahead? Prayer then can become difficult at best and almost impossible at worst. Even believing that there is a God at all can be very challenging. When we call out in anguish, it often seems that all we hear back is silence. This silence can be the most isolating and lonely of experiences.

Illness can seem like a desert island, where you are the only inhabitant. It is a place where you go alone. Although accompanied some of the way by those who love and care for you, it is a journey that you must make alone. You, and only you, can inhabit this space that is your illness. Others may have some idea, some inkling as to how you are feeling and what you are going through – they too may have experienced or are experiencing illness themselves – but your illness is unique; your illness is a one-off, never-before-experienced reality. You, with your own unique body, your own unique personality, your own unique psychology, your own unique spirituality, will experience the reality of your illness journey uniquely. This is the loneliness of illness. The seemingly in-this-on-your-own reality can be a very scary place indeed.

The fear and loneliness that come with illness are compounded by the severity of the illness. If your illness is serious but will pass with time, and you can see a clear route to wholeness again, then the loneliness, although real, may be short lived. However, if the prognosis is uncertain and the outcome of your illness is unsure, then that loneliness is compounded and can seem suffocating. It is at times like this that faith in God, trusting in God, believing in the reality of God's presence can, as I have said, seem nigh on impossible. What do you do then? To whom do you reach out and how? Where do you find solace or comfort? These are all good and honest questions to ask. When you cry out in the night from the depths of despair within yourself, and all you hear is silence, where then do you turn?

Without being too simplistic, you turn back to God, and you cry out to him. He is there. He exists. He has not abandoned you or left you alone. When it seemed on the cross as if Jesus had been completely abandoned by his Father, and he cried out, 'My God, My God, why have you forsaken me?', we know that the Father was nearest to him in the most intimate and precious way. This starkly honest cry from the heart of Jesus is his act of deepest faith in his Father. It is heard by the one who loves him most and who has not abandoned him. If you feel abandoned and alone, make this cry your cry. Do not be afraid to call out in a starkly honest way, 'My God, my God, why have you abandoned me?' For in doing so, you are expressing, in a most profound way, your faith in God the Father and an invitation for him to enter your heart in the same way he entered the heart of his dearly beloved son.

Prayer

Lord God,

I am so scared. I am so lonely. I have no resources left. Where are you? I feel so alone and helpless. I cannot go on much longer. I am so tired, so depleted, so empty. (Share honestly with God how you are feeling right now.) Lord, are you there? Lord, do you exist? Lord, why have you abandoned me? Why have you let this happen to me? Please, please help me. Please, please give me just a small crumb of solace, a small crumb of comfort. Please show yourself to me, even the tiniest glimpse, so that I can have something to hold onto. Please do not leave me alone like this. I cannot do this on my own. I desperately need your help. Please do not delay but come to me now. (Pause now to welcome the Father into your heart.) Amen.

2. Reach Out to Him

The Woman with the Haemorrhage
Mark 5:25–34

There was a woman afflicted with haemorrhages for twelve years. She had suffered greatly at the hands of many doctors and had spent all that she had. Yet she was not helped but only grew worse. She had heard about Jesus and came up behind him in the crowd and touched his cloak. She said, 'If I but touch his clothes, I shall be cured.' Immediately her flow of blood dried up. She felt in her body that she was healed of her affliction. Jesus, aware at once that power had gone out from him, turned around in the crowd and asked, 'Who has touched my clothes?' But his disciples said to him, 'You see how the crowd is pressing upon you, and yet you ask, "Who touched me?"' And he looked around to see who had done it. The woman, realising what had happened to her, approached in fear and trembling. She fell down before Jesus and told

> him the whole truth. He said to her, 'Daughter, your faith has saved you. Go in peace and be cured of your affliction.'

What line or phrase stands out for you as you read this passage? Take a quiet moment to dwell on this line or phrase, asking the Holy Spirit to heal you through it.

Reflection

What a powerful and touching passage this is from Mark's gospel. An ordinary, decent woman is afflicted for such a long while with an illness that had robbed her not only of her life's savings, but it seems every bit of her energy and strength as well. She was at the end of her tether, her wits' end. She had tried everything. She had gone to every doctor and had tried everything that had been recommended to her and yet she was feeling no better. Her isolation and loneliness are palpable. Twelve long and painful years and no end in sight. However, even after this long and trying time, she still carried within herself the hope and the dream that one day things would be better, that one day she would meet or find someone who would not only understand her reality, but who would heal her of her infirmity.

She had heard about Jesus. She had heard that he was a miracle worker. She had heard that he was a man of compassion for the poor and the sick. She had heard that he was a source of healing and strength. What had she got to lose? She was at her lowest; the only way was up. Jesus could be the key to unlock her healing, the answer to her prayer of twelve years.

'If I could but touch his clothes' is one of the greatest leaps of faith in the gospels and indeed in the history of faith. You could argue that as she had nothing to lose, it was an easy act of faith. However, if you have been let down time and time again, your ability to trust or get your hopes up is often depleted. For fear that you would be let down again, it is easier to build up a shell and cut yourself off. This did not happen to this woman. She reached out and touched Jesus through the crowds. It was a spontaneous act of trust that came straight from her heart.

This simple gesture brought her healing and wholeness. God doesn't expect us to do acrobatics or the impossible. A simple gesture of outreach to God, whatever our means, can become a gateway to healing and peace. In this very moment, this woman knew she wasn't on her own. Jesus was with her at the lowest ebb of her life and transformed this moment into one of healing. Even if she had not been physically healed, she knew in that moment that Jesus was with her. He was aware of her presence through her healing touch and he wanted her to know that he knew.

When we cry out in the depths of illness, no matter what way we manage it, even if we are not physically healed, we will, with God's grace, become aware of the presence of the one who knows us, who understands us, who loves us and who has compassion for us. In this moment, the veil of darkness falls away. In this moment, the hurt of isolation begins to lessen. In this moment, our loneliness is pierced through and we know he is with us. From where you are now, reach out and touch the hem of Jesus' garment. Do it using words or even simply by holding out your hands in a gesture of hope to the one who wants you to know that he is with you. Whatever way you can, and no matter how it looks, find a way to express your desire to be united in love with Jesus the healer. Take some time with this. Allow him to make his presence felt.

Prayer

Lord Jesus,

I have reached my lowest ebb. I am exhausted from the unending severity of this illness. I don't know where to go or to whom I should turn. (Share with the Lord how you are feeling right now.) The people in my life are amazing. They could not do more for me. Yet this does not feel like it is enough. Only you are enough. Only you can transform this experience of mine. Nothing and no one else can. Yet I am not sure how to reach out to you. I am not sure how I can begin to show you how much I need and depend on you. All I can say is please, please help me. That's all I can muster up. All I ask, if I cannot be physically healed, is to know your presence in my time of need. That's all I ask. Please show yourself to me in the darkness of this moment. I ask this through Christ our Lord. Amen.

3. Jesus, the Light of the World

The Man Born Blind

John 9:1–7

As he passed by he saw a man blind from birth. His disciples asked him, 'Rabbi, who sinned, this man or his parents, that he was born blind?' Jesus answered, 'Neither he nor his parents sinned; it is so that the works of God might be made visible through him. We have to do the works of the one who sent me while it is day. Night is coming when no one can work. While I am in the world, I am the light of the world.' When he had said this, he spat on the ground and made clay with the saliva, and smeared the clay on his eyes, and said to him, 'Go wash in the Pool of Siloam' (which means Sent). So he went and washed, and came back able to see.

What line or phrase stands out for you as you read this passage? Take a quiet moment to dwell on this line or phrase, asking the Holy Spirit to heal you through it.

Reflection

No one wants to be ill. No one wants to be unwell. We all strive to be well and healthy. We live in a world that celebrates health and strength. Thankfully, many are blessed with health and strength at this present time. However, illness and infirmity are a reality also. They come to us all at one time or another in our lives. Some experience illness throughout their lives while others only occasionally or near the end of their lives. Illness and infirmity are part of the human condition.

The fact that you are unwell is not a curse from God. God is not punishing you for anything you have done in your life, no matter how sinful your life has been. In Old Testament times, anyone who was sick, unwell or had some other misfortune was believed to have been struck down by God because of their own personal sinfulness or the sinfulness of their parents. Jesus changed all this. In the passage above, when asked who sinned for this man to be born blind, Jesus answers that neither this man nor his parents sinned, but that this illness happened so that the works of God might be displayed in him.

Illness and infirmity are not a cross sent to us by God to punish us. Let me say this again. Illness and infirmity are not a cross sent to us by God to punish us. Sometimes, when a person afflicted by illness looks back over their life and scans the horizon of their past, what often stands out for them are the moments when they gave in to weakness, temptation and sin. These sinful moments become a hook on which to hang the blame of God. It helps the person make sense of what has happened and gives them something to link their illness to. But this is not the reality of our God. He is not saving up our sins so that he can punish us with illness. He is not taking notice of our indiscretions so that he can inflict pain or misery. What we can say is that God allows illness, pain and suffering to take place in our lives. He allows it not to punish us, but to be true to the reality of illness in the world. People get sick. People become infirm. People become physically weak.

However, just because God allows pain and suffering does not mean that he has abandoned the person who is sick. It does not mean that he is not compassionate and caring. Going back to the story of the blind man, Jesus says that the man's blindness was allowed to happen so that 'the works of God might be made visible through him' (Jn 9:3). Through this man's faith and trust in God, God could reveal his power and his glory to the world. In healing this man of his blindness, the power of a loving and relieving God could be displayed to the world. Our faith and trust in God during illness, even the slightest and smallest amount of faith, can be all the Lord needs to reveal his power and his glory in and through our illness. Even the ability to hold on in the face of pain or suffering are signs of a powerful God who loves and cares for us. Without this powerful presence of God, we might go under, sink into despair and lose all hope. When the odds are stacked against us, God's simple, strong, abiding presence, revealed through our clinging on in illness, can truly show the glory of God in a real and tangible way. How do you feel you are holding on today?

Prayer

Dear Lord,

Though I am clinging on, I am haunted by my past. The sins and weaknesses of times gone by loom strong before my eyes and I am tempted to believe that this illness of mine is punishment for them all. Please heal me of this untruth. Please be with me now. (Share memories of the sins that trouble you.) Please strengthen me now. Please help me to know that you are with me now. Give me the grace to get through this day and to let these memories go. To survive today is enough for me, but I cannot do it on my own. Help me to believe that my meagre faith today is all that you need to reveal your glory in my life and to the whole world. Give me strength, Lord. Help me cope, Lord. Reveal your glory, Lord. Amen.

4. 'My Soul is Sorrowful even to Death'

The Agony in the Garden
Matthew 26:36–46

Then Jesus came with them to a place called Gethsemane, and he said to his disciples, 'Sit here while I go over there and pray.' He took along Peter and the two sons of Zebedee, and began to feel sorrow and distress. Then he said to them, 'My soul is sorrowful even to death. Remain here and keep watch with me.' He advanced a little and fell prostrate in prayer, saying, 'My Father, if it is possible, let this cup pass from me; yet, not as I will, but as you will.' When he returned to his disciples, he found them asleep. He said to Peter, 'So you could not keep watch with me for one hour? Watch and pray that you may not undergo the test. The spirit is willing, but the flesh is weak.' Withdrawing a second time, he prayed again, 'My Father, if it is not possible that this cup pass without my drinking it, your will be done!' Then he returned once more and found them asleep, for they could not keep their eyes open. He left them and withdrew again and prayed a third time, saying the same thing again. Then he returned to his disciples and said to them, 'Are you still sleeping and taking your rest? Behold, the hour is at hand when the Son of Man is to be handed over to sinners. Get up, let us go. Look, my betrayer is at hand.'

What line or phrase stands out for you as you read this passage? Take a quiet moment to dwell on this line or phrase, asking the Holy Spirit to heal you through it.

Reflection

When life is good, and your health is well, more often than not you don't think about illness or sickness. You may sympathise with and have compassion for those around you who are sick, but you don't imagine yourself being sick. You just get on with things. This is the way it should be. Life is to be lived and enjoyed. However, when illness and infirmity come your way, you are plunged into the reality of what it means to be weak and frail. The sicker and frailer you are, the more distant the memory of what it was like to be well becomes. You are surrounded by a wall of sickness that is all encompassing, that colours everything. It is like you are in a prison of illness and you cannot find the door out. You become helpless, dependent and vulnerable. It is not an easy place to be.

This feeling of helplessness and vulnerability is compounded further if the illness is serious, life-threatening or terminal. At this time, one can truly relate to Jesus as he was in the Garden of Gethsemane. Here in this garden, plunged into the dark night of betrayal, it would seem that Jesus, in the loneliness of this moment, is searching for meaning, for understanding of what is happening, so that he may be able to accept it. Anyone who has been or is seriously ill can truly relate to his words, 'My soul is sorrowful even to death' (Mt 26:38). Jesus, aware of the fate that awaits him, very humanly feels the pain of this burden to the greatest extent. As human, as well as divine, he will have to face the grave and painful journey to Calvary alone. Do these words, 'My soul is sorrowful even to death,' echo in your heart? Take a moment now to hear them. Try to take comfort from the fact the Jesus himself echoed these words. You are not alone.

Seeing this road stretching out ahead of him, Jesus cries out in a deeply sorrowful way, 'My Father, if it is not possible that this cup pass without my drinking it, your will be done!' (Mt 26:42). Can you relate to these words of Jesus? Do you deeply desire that the cup that is placed before you pass you by? Do you find it hard to say the words that Jesus says, 'Your will be done'? This is most natural. It is understandable. God understands where you are coming from, and he does not condemn you, but loves you all the deeper.

Travelling the road of illness and infirmity is a lonely, often terrifying journey. No one else truly understands what you are going through. And yet God knows what you are going through. God has walked that road. He has experienced the fear, the pain, the isolation, the loneliness, the anxiety and the sheer terror. The God we believe in is not aloof or distant to us. He completely understands our plight and understands what we need to get through it. He is on hand to offer us the strength we need to walk this road. As he walked it with dignity, he teaches us how to walk with dignity. His ear is open to hear us call out in honesty, in fear, in desperation from the isolation of our pain. He treats us with the respect of listening to our hearts. He wants us to know that within the pain of our illness he is with us, closer than our very selves, uniting his heart with ours in a bond of pure love.

How are you feeling now? What are the thoughts and feelings inside you? Share them now in an honest and real way with God. Hold nothing back. Scream if you have to. Sob if it comes. Beg if it is the only way you can express how you are feeling. But don't keep it bottled up inside. God wants us always to share in an honest way the burdens of our lives. He wants us to open our hearts to him, warts and all. For it is by opening our hearts that we invite, allow and welcome the God of healing love into our very being. Our honesty, then, is our gift of permission to God to be with us in a real and substantial way. We should never be afraid, embarrassed or slow to be truly honest with God. Honesty is the path to true encounter with your God. Can you be honest with God now in these quiet moments?

Prayer

Lord God,

I cry out to you in my need from the very depths of my heart. I need you desperately. I am so weak and frail. I have no energy left. I am terrified and feel so very much alone. I cry out to you the words that you called out to your Father: 'My soul is sorrowful even to death.' Lord God, please hear my cry. Please understand my plea. Please take it to your heart. (Cry out to him now in your own words.) Please give me the courage and strength I need for this moment of my life. Be with me in an intimate way so that I can truly know your presence and your love.

5. 'Father, into your Hands I Commend my Spirit'

The Death of Jesus

Luke 23:44–47

It was now about noon and darkness came over the whole land until three in the afternoon because of an eclipse of the sun. Then the veil of the temple was torn down the middle. Jesus cried out in a loud voice, 'Father, into your hands I commend my spirit'; and when he had said this he breathed his last. The centurion who witnessed what had happened glorified God and said, 'This man was innocent beyond doubt.'

What line or phrase stands out for you as you read this passage? Take a quiet moment to dwell on this line or phrase, asking the Holy Spirit to heal you through it.

Reflection

Serious or terminal illness is a huge mountain to climb. It depletes every morsel of energy, every personal reserve that a human being has. However, it cannot deplete or erode a person's dignity or worth. Though a person's health may deteriorate, their dignity does not. The one who is sick is, at every stage of their illness, a beloved, precious human being created by God out of complete and total love. They may feel like a burden on others. They may be dependent on others. They may feel completely helpless. But they are no less an incredible work of art created by God. At times, this can be so hard to believe. When a person is helpless and dependent, they can feel utterly lost and useless and, when things are really tough, can even wish it were all over.

In these times, finding the strength to pray can be very difficult. It can be hard to pray even when there are no heavy burdens on a person, let alone when things are weighing heavily on them. In these challenging moments, just forming words that might even resemble a prayer to God can be too much. However, this does not mean that there is no prayer going on.

Even when we cannot pray, the Holy Spirit prays through us. The Holy Spirit makes up for whatever we lack, whatever we are not able to say ourselves. Our task during these difficult times is simply to keep our eyes fixed on God. For God is always gazing lovingly on us, even when we don't realise or appreciate that he is. God never stops loving and caring for us. He sustains us in ways that are often impossible to recognise. When we are struggling and in pain, our loving God and creator feels our pain with us and shows us the deepest compassion. If it is even possible, he loves us all the more in our dependency. God our Heavenly Father never, I repeat, never abandons his children. It is not possible. He understands when we cannot pray in a way we would like. With God there is no condemnation, only love – the love of a parent for a child. Think about this for a minute. Allow this reality to speak to your heart. Welcome the Father's love for you into the darkest recesses of your heart. Allow God our Father to make his home in you.

From the moment he set out for Jerusalem, and maybe even much earlier than that, Jesus was acutely aware that his journey would lead to the cross. Imagine now the reality of this: Jesus, the Son of God, fully human, fully divine, was aware that he was headed to his death – a cruel and painful death at the hands of sinners. How did Jesus cope with the reality of this? What gave him the strength he needed to face the horror of the cross? Well, put simply, but not naively, Jesus kept his eyes fixed on and his heart united with his Father in heaven. The bond he had with his Father sustained him in every moment and at every step. He drew enormous strength from the real and tangible love gifted to him by his Father. This is summed up in this most powerful line uttered by Jesus on the cross: 'Father, into your hands I commend my spirit.' These words speak volumes. The confidence Jesus had in his Father shone through. He was telling the world that at the lowest and most difficult ebb of life his Father can be trusted, can be depended on and will not let you down. Can you find it in your heart now, at this moment, to utter these words yourself, 'Father, into your hands I commend my spirit'? Take a moment now to try to speak these words. Even if you have trouble believing, accepting or trusting in these words, try to say them. In the very utterance of these words you allow the power of our loving God to enter into the reality of your situation.

Prayer

Lord God,

I am desperate. My strength and my energy are gone. I have reached the lowest point in my life. I cannot pray. I cannot find the energy or the words. Just to exist now is hard enough. The only words I can utter are the words of your son, Jesus: 'Father, into your hands I commend my spirit.' Please, please hear these words. Please, please help me. Please, please don't allow me to sink beneath the waves. Hold my head up and help me through this hour. Amen.

6. 'Jesus, Have Pity on Me'

The Blind Bartimaeus

Mark 10:46–52

They came to Jericho. And as he was leaving Jericho with his disciples and a sizable crowd, Bartimaeus, a blind man, the son of Timaeus, sat by the roadside begging. On hearing that it was Jesus of Nazareth, he began to cry out and say, 'Jesus, son of David, have pity on me.' And many rebuked him, telling him to be silent. But he kept calling out all the more, 'Son of David, have pity on me.' Jesus stopped and said, 'Call him.' So they called the blind man, saying to him, 'Take courage; get up, he is calling you.' He threw aside his cloak, sprang up, and came to Jesus. Jesus said to him in reply, 'What do you want me to do for you?' The blind man replied to him, 'Master, I want to see.' Jesus told him, 'Go your way; your faith has saved you.'

> Immediately he received his sight and followed him on the way.

What line or phrase stands out for you as you read this passage? Take a quiet moment to dwell on this line or phrase, asking the Holy Spirit to heal you through it.

Reflection

As I have said earlier, when a person is ill or infirm, they can be lost for words. This can be especially true when they are weakened and frail. How are they to pray? What kind of words can they use? They wonder to themselves as they endeavour to pray, must I put on a brave face and use brave words and speak in a 'nice way' towards God? We often think that when we pray we must use happy words and joyful themes in our prayer. This can be particularly difficult if you are feeling anything but joyful, anything but happy. There is truly something artificial in prayer when our heart and our body is feeling in a certain way and yet we feel that we must put on an 'act' in the face of God. We may even feel that it would be disrespectful to tell God how we really feel, what we really desire, how we would desire him to reveal himself in our lives.

Real prayer is honest prayer. Real prayer is telling God what is going on in our lives and in our hearts, warts and all. Real prayer is holding nothing back. Real prayer is not looking for the polite and safe words, but should be an attempt, even a feeble attempt, to reveal our hearts truly as they are before our God. Sometimes we have to shout at God. Sometimes we have to give out to God. Sometimes we have to beg from God. Sometimes we have to weep before our God. Sometimes we just have to remain silent before him. Think of someone you truly love, someone you admire and trust. Would that person prefer you to put on an act when you are in their presence? Would they not be more likely to pick up from your demeanour and tone of voice that you were sad and upset even though you might have told them that all is well? I am sure they would prefer to hear from you how you actually are. By being real with someone we love, we grow in trust and respect for each other.

Take some time now to tell God how you are feeling and what is going on in your heart. Don't try to dress it up in 'nice' language. It doesn't have to conform to a certain formula. It just has to be real. Finish by inviting the healing presence of God into the reality that is your life. Sit in silence in the presence of the one who accepts, who loves and who understands.

Prayer

Lord God,

This is how I am feeling now. (Reveal honestly to God how you are feeling. Hold nothing back.)

Thank you, Lord, for allowing me the dignity to be honest with you, to tell you how I really am. I have been hiding these things from you out of (name why you were holding back from being honest with God, for example fear, embarrassment, insecurity, etc.). Now I know that I can be real with you and honest and open in your presence. I know, dear Lord, that what I have shared with you, you treat with the greatest respect.

Take all my worries and concerns to your heart, I pray, and transform them and me. Fill me, I pray, with peace, hope, security and love. Give me the strength I need this day, this hour and this minute. Thank you, Lord. Amen.

7. 'Do Not Weep'

Raising of the Widow's Son

Luke 7:11–17

Soon afterward he journeyed to a city called Nain, and his disciples and a large crowd accompanied him. As he drew near to the gate of the city, a man who had died was being carried out, the only son of his mother, and she was a widow. A large crowd from the city was with her. When the Lord saw her, he was moved with pity for her and said to her, 'Do not weep.' He stepped forward and touched the coffin; at this the bearers halted, and he said, 'Young man, I tell you, arise!' The dead man sat up and began to speak, and Jesus gave him to his mother. Fear seized them all, and they glorified God, exclaiming, 'A great prophet has arisen in our midst,' and 'God has visited his people.' This report about him spread through the whole of Judea and in all the surrounding region.

What line or phrase stands out for you as you read this passage? Take a quiet moment to dwell on this line or phrase, asking the Holy Spirit to heal you through it.

Reflection

As I have said before, Illness can be a very lonely place. Hopefully, you can get all the care and help you need from your doctors, nurses, carers, family and friends – though they can only travel with you for a certain distance. It is you who has to carry the burden; you who has to try to make sense of what is happening; you who, in the darkness of the night, or the quietness of your room, has to face the reality of what is happening to you. Yes, illness can be a very lonely place indeed.

This loneliness can be hugely magnified if you feel that God is distant from you or has deserted you. If and when this happens, you can feel like the smallest and most insignificant person in the world. Your health has failed you and now you feel that God has failed you too. But has he? Let us look at the evidence we have from the scriptures to see how Jesus approaches and deals with people who feel insignificant and small.

You have just read the words from Luke's gospel in which Jesus enters the town of Nain. Nain is a small and insignificant town in itself. It is a tiny village which would only be a small dot on a map. The size of the town itself indicates that there is no place that is outside the power and love of God. Indeed, it is in places such as Nain that Jesus made the greatest impact. Here, Jesus comes across a funeral procession that is making its way out of the town. It is a small gathering, but a significant one, as the person being buried is a young man. This is a tragedy. We don't know how he died; we just know that his dead body is on a stretcher, being carried to the cemetery. As the story unfolds, the sadness and the enormity of this funeral become more evident. The young man is the only son of his mother, and his mother is a widow. A widow. This is huge. Widows were, in the time of our Lord, the most vulnerable and the most at-risk members of the community. They could not work. They could receive no benefits from the state. They were helpless. They depended on a son or daughter to care for them or provide for them. However, in this story the only one who could help was now dead. This widow's plight was enormous; her future most precarious.

As she weeps for the loss of her son and for her uncertain future, even without calling out to Jesus, Jesus comes up to her and enters into the reality of her situation. Jesus is filled with the deepest compassion and love for her. He understands her plight. He reaches forward and stops the procession. He calls to the young man and tells him to get up, and, when he arises, he gives him back to his mother. He gives this woman back her son, her security, her future. In that moment, her deepest sadness and despair are turned to her greatest joy and hope.

We too can be filled with the great hope and joy flowing from this story. It speaks clearly and loudly to the fact that God notices everything and everyone. He especially notices those who feel most insignificant and small, those who feel the world has forgotten them. As you read this, how do you feel? Do you feel small, insignificant, abandoned, alone or frustrated? Allow whatever you are feeling to surface. If you can find it in yourself, share these feelings with God. If you can't find it in you to speak these words in prayer, know now that God hears them, notices them and reverences them. They are your unique gift to your

God today. They are probably to the most precious gift you will ever give your God. Take time in silence welcoming his healing power.

Prayer

Lord God,
In my helplessness, I ask you to draw near to me. In my isolation and pain, I ask you to come through the crowd and make your presence felt. As the grieving widow who had lost her son was swamped by pain and you approached her in love, so now do I ask you to see my pain and grief and approach me with the greatest love. It is now more than ever that I need you close, now more than ever I need to feel your presence. Please reach into the darkness and pain of my life and reveal yourself to me in a way that I can know. (Use your own words here to express your desire to experience his love in your life now.) Lord, you have shown your presence in the past. I pray that you show your presence now in the midst of all that is happening to me. Amen.

8. 'O Woman, Great is your Faith!'

The Canaanite Woman's Faith

Matthew 15:21–28

Then Jesus went from that place and withdrew to the region of Tyre and Sidon. And behold, a Canaanite woman of that district came and called out, 'Have pity on me, Lord, Son of David! My daughter is tormented by a demon.' But he did not say a word in answer to her. His disciples came and asked him, 'Send her away, for she keeps calling out after us.' He said in reply, 'I was sent only to the lost sheep of the house of Israel.' But the woman came and did him homage, saying, 'Lord, help me.' He said in reply, 'It is not right to take the food of the children and throw it to the dogs.' She said, 'Please, Lord, for even the dogs eat the scraps that fall from the table of their masters.' Then Jesus said to her in reply, 'O woman, great is your faith! Let it be done for you as you wish.' And her daughter was healed from that hour.

What line or phrase stands out for you as you read this passage? Take a quiet moment to dwell on this line or phrase, asking the Holy Spirit to heal you through it.

Reflection

Illness and infirmity rob us of every ounce of energy and strength that we have. Even the strongest and most powerful people are humbled and laid low by serious illness. As our energy levels and physical strength begin to wane, so too often does our ability to remain positive. Even spiritually we can reach an all-time low, finding not even the strength to pray. This in its turn erodes our ability to trust and have faith in God. The sense of running on empty is a real one that affects us in real ways. Even our ability to believe that God exists is challenged. This can lead to despair and a sense of hopelessness.

Where is God? Is there a God? Why have I been left like this? These are all substantial questions. We are obliged to ask them of God when and if they arise.

God is not beyond our questioning. God is big enough to take our questions onto himself and hold them close to his heart. These are trying and confusing times. This is the dark night. However, we must not allow this darkness to engulf us. We must not allow ourselves to be overwhelmed into despair. We must not allow ourselves to fall into hopelessness. We must grit our teeth and hold firm in the face of darkness.

The Canaanite woman we have just read about didn't allow the enormity of what was happening to her daughter to lead her to despair. When seemingly met by Jesus with silence and indifference, she cried all the more. When challenged by Jesus as to whether or not her daughter deserved to be healed or not, the woman dug deep and stuck to her guns. Jesus was the one who was going to heal her daughter and bring her to wholeness – she was sure of that. Her tenacity and fortitude shone forth from a most trying experience. She teaches us today never to give up hope, never to give in to despair and never to lose trust in our God. The message that screams out from this story to all who are in need is clear. It is simply this: Dig deep. Do not give up hope. Keep your heart, your faith and your trust in Jesus. Do not take 'no' as an answer from him, but return often to him and implore his mercy.

What Jesus does here seems, on the face of it, to be cruel and uncaring. He seems insensitive and unapproachable. However, as we dig deeper into this story, we quickly realise that Jesus was acting this way not to shake the woman's faith, but to affirm it, strengthen it and allow it to flourish. What emerges from this woman's heart is a faith that maybe even she herself never knew existed. From the depths of her being, Jesus drew out a faith that not only led to her daughter's healing, but to this woman's being used for generations unending as an example of what can come about and be achieved if a person remains true to their belief and their trust in God. Little did this woman know that the faith that she held as a Canaanite woman, a woman from whom such faith would not have been expected, would be celebrated as a beacon of hope shining through a dark and difficult experience.

Draw some comfort and courage from the example of the Canaanite woman. Notice what she says and does. Allow her faith to strengthen yours. Allow her resolve to keep going to help you to keep going. Let the example of her life and her faith give you the courage you need not to give up, not to throw in the towel. As she kept her resolve, so you too keep your resolve. Jesus is listening. He is present. He hears you. He is allowing you to realise just how strong your faith is even in these difficult times.

Prayer

Dear Lord,

I am here. I am calling out to you. I am not going away. I am not going to leave you or turn my back on you. Even though I am challenged so deeply this day, I am not going to give up hope in you but the opposite. I call all the more loudly. I scream all the more ferociously. I need you now. I need your healing now. I deeply desire to feel your healing presence in my life. Do not let me down. Do not let me cry in vain. Do not let the darkness of this moment overcome me. Jesus, my Saviour, my Lord, I trust in you. I love you. I need you. Please do not let me down. Shine through this experience in my life so that others may come to believe that you are one who can be trusted, who can be believed, who can be loved. Amen.

9. 'Behold, your Mother'

Mary by the Cross

John 19:25–27

Standing by the cross of Jesus were his mother and his mother's sister, Mary the wife of Clopas, and Mary of Magdala. When Jesus saw his mother and the disciple there whom he loved, he said to his mother, 'Woman, behold, your son.' Then he said to the disciple, 'Behold, your mother.' And from that hour the disciple took her into his home.

What line or phrase stands out for you as you read this passage? Take a quiet moment to dwell on this line or phrase, asking the Holy Spirit to heal you through it.

Reflection

Imagine for a moment what the last earthly journey of Jesus through the streets of Jerusalem must have been like. He had been betrayed, handed over, given an unfair trial before Pilate and now he is headed for the cross. Those final moments of his earthly journey were filled with pain. He was mocked. The crowds looked on him as a criminal. Imagine the isolation and loneliness of those moments of agony. They even grabbed a reluctant Simon of Cyrene from the crowd to help him carry his cross. They did so not merely to aid Jesus on his journey and make things easier for him, but to ensure that he wouldn't die before he got to the 'main event': his crucifixion on Calvary. I'm sure Simon wished they had picked on someone else and not him. If only he was able to go on his way without being caught up in all this. No one wanted to come under the attention or eye of the Romans. I'm sure Simon couldn't wait to get to Calvary so that he could get out of there. This is a sad, pathetic and painful scene.

Jesus was well and truly alone … Or was he? No. Mary his mother was there. She had been with him from the very first moment of his existence and she bore him in her womb. She had welcomed him into the world as her son. She, with Joseph, had cared for, washed, clothed, taught, but most of all loved Jesus incredibly. She was the greatest mother who journeyed with her beloved son; there at every step, from the simplest to the most profound. From the first miracle at Cana in Galilee to his last breath on the cross. The image of Mary holding her beloved son in her arms after he was taken from the cross stands out in history as one of the most poignant of all.

Mary did not run away. She did not abandon. She loved to the end. She could have been forgiven for turning away from this cruel scene, but she didn't. She couldn't. She wouldn't. Imagine the comfort Mary gave to Jesus as he hung from the cross, as he looked her in the eye and knew she was there with him.

Mary is our mother too. As she did for Jesus, she does for us. She, like her son, is with us at every step of our journey, present with a mother's compassionate love. She is unperturbed. She is resolute. She does not abandon or turn her back on our pain, but looks ever more lovingly at us to reassure us not just of her presence, but also of the presence of her son Jesus. Mary is sent to us by Jesus to be our companion on the road of illness. No matter how serious our illness is, Mary is close. We can be sure of her presence.

Take a moment now to become aware of Mary's presence in your life today. Become aware of a mother's love, holding you as she held her son. From her place in heaven with her son, she intercedes for us in a most profound way. Allow now her compassionate love to seep deeply into your wounded and pained heart. Ask her now to intercede for you with her son. Ask her to take your prayers and place them in the heart of her son. Allow her to be your dearest companion through the darkness and pain of your illness. Allow Mary our Mother to accompany you as you journey to the light of her only begotten son.

Speak now to Mary as your mother. Share with her your cares and your worries. Allow her to hold your hand and lead you to her son.

Prayer

Dear Lord,
Thank you for your beautiful and compassionate mother. Thank you for allowing her to enter deeply into my pain and sadness at this moment in my life. Thank you for allowing her to reveal to me a mother's love so that this present journey is not travelled alone. As I need you today to heal me, I need her today to soothe and comfort me. I am

never alone while you and your mother Mary are with me. Please reassure me now and comfort me in this present moment. Allow your mother Mary to hold me in her loving embrace. Thank you, Lord. Thank you, Mary. Amen.

10. A Reflection for a Carer

The Healing of a Paralytic
Luke 5:17–26

One day as Jesus was teaching, Pharisees and teachers of the law were sitting there who had come from every village of Galilee and Judea and Jerusalem, and the power of the Lord was with him for healing. And some men brought on a stretcher a man who was paralysed; they were trying to bring him in and set him in his presence. But not finding a way to bring him in because of the crowd, they went up on the roof and lowered him on the stretcher through the tiles into the middle in front of Jesus. When he saw their faith, he said, 'As for you, your sins are forgiven.' Then the scribes and Pharisees began to ask themselves, 'Who is this who speaks blasphemies? Who but God alone can forgive sins?' Jesus knew their thoughts and said to them in reply, 'What are you thinking in your hearts? Which is easier, to say, "Your sins are forgiven," or to say, "Rise and walk"? But that you may know that the Son of Man has authority on earth to forgive sins' – he said to the man who was paralysed, 'I say to you, rise, pick up your stretcher, and go home.' He stood up immediately before them, picked up what he had been lying on, and went home, glorifying God. Then astonishment seized them all and they glorified God, and, struck with awe, they said, 'We have seen incredible things today.'

Reflection

When illness and infirmity befall someone we love, it can be a heart-breaking, shocking, helpless and frustrating experience. No one wants to see someone they love in pain or suffering. Standing by, watching someone we love suffer and not knowing how to help can be very draining. This is particularly true if the illness being suffered is a serious, painful or long-standing one. We all try to help one another in times of need, but what happens when the help that we have to offer seems utterly inadequate? This can be an isolating and lonely place to be and can lead to a deep suffering on the part of the carer. They can feel that they are letting the one they love down in their moment of greatest need. Caring for one who is sick is one of the hardest acts of love one person can show another, because it often feels that what is being offered for the sick person is never enough. The carer can feel like a spectator, looking in on the misery of another and not being able, it would seem, to do very much. Out of compassion for the sick person, they often have the wish to take some of the pain and illness onto themselves instead. They can also feel that they could and should be doing more. 'If only I could do more' becomes the predominant thought in their mind.

Caring for a sick person long term can be exhausting for the carer. They can be worn down from the seemingly twenty-four-hours-a-day pressure that comes from looking after a person who is ill. Taken to the extreme, the act of caring itself can cause the carer to become ill also. They can be under so much mental stress that it begins to take a toll on their body. They too can find that prayer becomes all the more difficult, as they too seem only to hear silence in response. They are on hand to listen to the cries and fears of the one who is sick, but who will sit with them and listen to the cries and fears that they too feel? The role of carer can be a lonely experience indeed. Hopefully, some of the earlier reflections on how to pray in times of illness will be of help to carers also. If they put themselves in the place of the one who is sick and read the reflections in that light, they too might find a way of expressing their deepest thoughts to God in prayer.

The men who took the paralysed man to Jesus were indeed heroic. They tried their best to bring him and place him before Jesus through the front door, but the crowds made that impossible. They looked for another way and found it by bringing him onto the roof and lowering him down through it before Jesus. They didn't give up on him when the first challenge arrived; they tried another way. They did their best for this man. They did all they could. And it was enough. No one could have asked for more from them. Whatever a carer can do for someone who is sick is enough. Think about this for a moment. Try your best to allow these words to sink into your heart. You are doing enough. Indeed, you will probably never really know just how profound an effect the care you are giving a sick person is having on their life. It takes an act of trust to know that it is enough. Try to let any fears of guilt or inadequacy go. Hand them over to the Lord and ask him to purify these fears and free you from them.

It is so important for the carer to take care of themselves. They need to sleep well, eat well and exercise well as best they can. They have an important role in taking care of themselves so that they can continue to care for the one who is sick. This means not feeling guilty if they have to ask for help, admit they are not coping, spend time on their own away from the sick person, take a few days respite, ask someone else to take over for a while, or take a break each day and do something for themselves. This is not selfishness. This is not a lack of generosity. This is being realistic and mature. Take a few moments now to reflect on your own situation as a carer. How is it really going? How are you really feeling? Are you taking enough care of yourself? Are there any small changes you can make that could elevate your self-care even a small bit?

If you can, share all this with the Lord in some quiet time of prayer. Share your heart with the ultimate carer, Jesus. For Jesus notices. He notices everything. He notices even the smallest, seemingly insignificant attempts to care for someone who is sick. He notices even a cup of water given in his name to another in need. Do you consider the cup of water you gave to someone who is sick significant? Take some time now to recognise the significance of that which seems insignificant. The reason why the gospel story of the healing of the paralysed man includes the details of him being carried, of him being lifted, of him being lowered down, is because they were noticed. They were important and not to be overlooked. They made all the difference to this man in need. Out of context, this story of carrying or lifting someone would not seem all that important; however, because they were genuine acts of kindness to a man in need, they carry a huge significance that cannot be glossed over. Every act of love to a sick person is an act of Christ. The carer is the eyes, the ears, the mouth, the hands and the feet of Christ. Indeed, they are the living and real heart of Christ to the one who is sick. The carer reveals the face of Jesus to the one who is sick.

We can go one step further. Every act of love and kindness shown to a sick person is shown to Christ. This is because the sick person is Christ. Christ is present first and foremost in the sick, the lonely, the downcast and the rejected. What we do for another, we do for him. Again, take a moment to reflect on the fact that the person you are caring for today is Christ. Overwhelming, isn't it? Humbling, isn't it? Yet, whatever you do for this one who is ill, you are doing for Christ, the Saviour of the World, and it will not go unnoticed or lack reward.

In Summary

Try to pray as best you can given the stress you are under. Try to share all your feelings, all your desires, all your hopes and all your frustrations with the Lord. It doesn't have to look pretty, but it needs to be real.

It is not just OK to take care of yourself, it is necessary. You owe it not only to yourself, but to the sick person also.

The Lord notices everything, even the smallest gesture or cup of water.

What you are doing for the sick person in your care, you are doing for Christ.

Prayer

Dear Lord,

I am trying my best. I am trying to care for N. to the best of my ability. I often feel like it is not enough. I often feel inadequate. I feel tired most of the time and lack the energy I feel I need to be really present to N. Help me. Strengthen me. Sustain me. Help me to understand that I am doing enough.

Lord, I often feel guilty if I steal some time for myself. I feel that I am letting N. down. Please free me from these feelings so that I won't start to resent N. in their sickness.

Lord, help me to realise most of all that what I do for N., I am doing for you. Help me to see your face in N's face and hear you in their voice.

Help all who care for others. Help and sustain us so that we just don't exist at this time, but live with joy, with hope and with peace.

(Add your own words here.)

I ask all this through Christ our Lord. Amen.